What Does a Sanitation Worker Do?

What Does a Community Helper Do?

Heather Miller

Words to Know

dumpster (DUHMP-stur)—
Large container used to hold
garbage.

garbage (GAR-big)—Food and
other things that are thrown
out.

refrigerator (reh-FRIG-uh-ray-
tur)—A device that keeps food
cold.

sanitation (san-i-TAY-shun)—
Keeping things free of
unhealthy things, like trash or
germs.

Enslow Elementary

an imprint of

Enslow Publishers, Inc.

40 Industrial Road	PO Box 38
Box 398	Aldershot
Berkeley Heights, NJ 07922	Hants GU12 6BP
USA	UK

http://www.enslow.com

Contents

Sanitation workers drive **garbage** trucks.

Garbage Day!

The street is quiet. It is still dark. Suddenly, *RUMBLE*, *RUMBLE*, *RUMBLE*! A big garbage truck drives down the road. It is garbage day in your neighborhood. There is a lot of trash!

Sanitation workers even clean up the streets of big cities.

Working in All Types of Weather

Sanitation workers work in all types of weather. They work in the hot sun. They work in cold snow. In rain, ice, or wind, sanitation workers must work to pick up the trash.

Piles of trash on curbs are picked up by sanitation workers.

Where Do Sanitation Workers Stop for Trash?

Sanitation workers stop at many places to pick up garbage. They drive through neighborhoods and stop at each house as they go. They empty dumpsters by stores, diners, shopping centers, and hospitals.

Sanitation workers lift heavy bags of trash into their trucks.

Picking Up Trash

Sanitation workers must be strong. They lift many heavy things. They carry garbage cans, boxes, and bags filled with trash. Sometimes, they even lift refrigerators!

Sanitation workers work together. In this small town in Vermont, trash is picked up and loaded onto a cart pulled by a horse.

Staying Safe

Sanitation workers must be careful when they work. Garbage can be slippery or sharp. Sanitation workers work together. They help keep one another safe.

Sanitation workers wear special clothes to keep them safe.

Thick gloves protect their hands from broken glass, sharp metal, and germs. Bright, colored vests help other drivers see sanitation workers who are working on the road. They even wear special hats to protect them on the job.

Garbage trucks go to the dump. The trucks unload all the trash.

Garbage Trucks

Sanitation workers drive trucks. Some trucks are big. Other trucks are small. Sanitation workers load them with garbage. They take the trucks to the dump when they are full. There, the trash is taken off the truck. Sanitation workers go back to pick up more garbage.

Raccoons and other animals hide in dumpsters. They look for piles of trash. Sanitation workers empty dumpsters so these animals stay away.

Helping the Community

People throw things away every day. If sanitation workers did not do their jobs, piles of trash would grow and grow.

Garbage is stinky and ugly. It can attract animals like rats and raccoons. These animals are dangerous to people and pets.

Every day, sanitation workers take garbage to the dump. They help keep our streets clean and safe.

RUMBLE, RUMBLE! **The next day, the garbage truck is back on the road. Sanitation workers work almost every day to keep their communities safe and clean. Sanitation workers are community heroes.**

Make Less Waste

How can you help make less waste? It is easy!

When you pack a lunch for school:
    Use a reusable lunch box or bag.
    Use containers you can use again.
    Take only what you know you will eat.

When you look for school supplies:
    Try pens and pencils you can refill.
    Try a sturdy backpack or book bag that
    will last a long time.
    Use up paper from the year before.

When you are at home:
    Use scrap paper to write notes.
    Use cloth napkins instead of paper ones.
    Help your family recycle.

For more tips, check out the "Creating Less
Trash at School" Web site on the next page.

Learn More

Books

LeBoutillier, Nate. *A Day in the Life of a Garbage Collector*. Mankato, Minn.: Capstone Press, 2005.

Maass, Robert. *Garbage*. New York: Henry Holt, 2000.

Macken, JoAnn Early. *Sanitation Worker*. Milwaukee, Wisc.: Weekly Reader Early Learning Library, 2003.

Internet Addresses

Adventures of the Garbage Gremlin
<http://www.epa.gov/epaoswer/non-hw/recycle/gremlin/gremlin.htm>
Visit a dump and learn about recycling with the Garbage Gremlin.

Creating Less Trash at School
<http://www.moea.state.mn.us/campaign/school/index.html>
Learn more about making less trash.

Index

Note to Teachers and Parents: The *What Does a Community Helper Do?* series supports curriculum standards for K–4 learning about community services and helpers. The Words to Know section introduces subject-specific vocabulary. Early readers may require help with these new words.

Series Literacy Consultant:
Allan A. De Fina, Ph.D.
Past President of the New Jersey Reading Association
Professor, Department of Literacy Education
New Jersey City University

Enslow Elementary, an imprint of Enslow Publishers, Inc.

Enslow Elementary® is a registered trademark
of Enslow Publishers, Inc.

Library of Congress Cataloging-in-Publication Data

Miller, Heather.
    What does a sanitation worker do? / Heather Miller.
        p. cm. — (What does a community helper do?)
    Includes bibliographical references and index.
    ISBN 0-7660-2543-8
    1. Sanitation workers—Juvenile literature. 2. Refuse
and refuse disposal—Juvenile literature. I. Title.
II. Series.
HD8039.S257M55 2005
363.72'023—dc22   2004006954

Printed in the United States of America

10 9 8 7 6 5 4 3 2 1

To Our Readers:
We have done our best to make sure all Internet Addresses in this book were active and appropriate when we went to press. However, the author and the publisher have no control over and assume no liability for the material available on those Internet sites or on other Web sites they may link to. Any comments or suggestions can be sent by e-mail to comments@enslow.com or to the address on the back cover.

Illustration Credits: Associated Press, pp. 4, 6, 8, 10, 12, 16, 18 (bottom), 20; Associated Press, Effingham Daily News, p. 18 (top); Associated Press, The Daily Reflector, p. 14; Hemera Technologies, Inc. 1997-2000, pp. 2, 15, 22 (top); © 2004 JupiterImages, p. 22 (middle and bottom); Punchstock, p. 1.

Cover Illustration: Punchstock (bottom); top left to right (photos 1, 2, and 4: Associated Press; photo 3: Associated Press, The Daily Reflector.)